Gangs and Weapons

TOOKIE SPEAKS OUT AGAINST GANG VIOLENCE™

Stanley "Tookie" Williams

with Barbara Cottman Becnel

The Rosen Publishing Group's
PowerKids Press™
New York

Published in 1996 by The Rosen Publishing Group, Inc.
29 East 21st Street, New York, NY 10010

First Edition

Book design: Kim Sonsky

Photo credits: Cover by Michael Brandt; front cover inset, back cover and p. 4 © J. Patrick Forden; p. 7 © Bill Stanton/International Stock; p. 8, 11, 15, 16, 20 by Sarah Friedman; p. 12 © Richard Pharoah/International Stock; p. 19 by Maria Moreno.

Williams, Stanley.
    Gangs and weapons / by Stanley "Tookie" Williams and Barbara Cottman Becnel.
        p.   cm. — (Tookie speaks out against gang violence)
    Includes index.
    Summary: Discusses the violence that can occur when gangs have guns.
    ISBN 0-8239-2342-8
    1. Gangs—United States—Juvenile literature. 2. Violence—United States—Prevention—Juvenile literature. 3. Firearms ownership—United States—Juvenile literature. [1. Gangs. 2. Violence. 3. Firearms ownership.] I. Becnel, Barbara Cottman. II. Title. III. Series: Williams, Stanley. Tookie speaks out against gang violence.
    HV6439.U5W74 1996
    364.1'06'60973—dc20   96-1510
                                                                                    CIP
                                                                                    AC

Contents

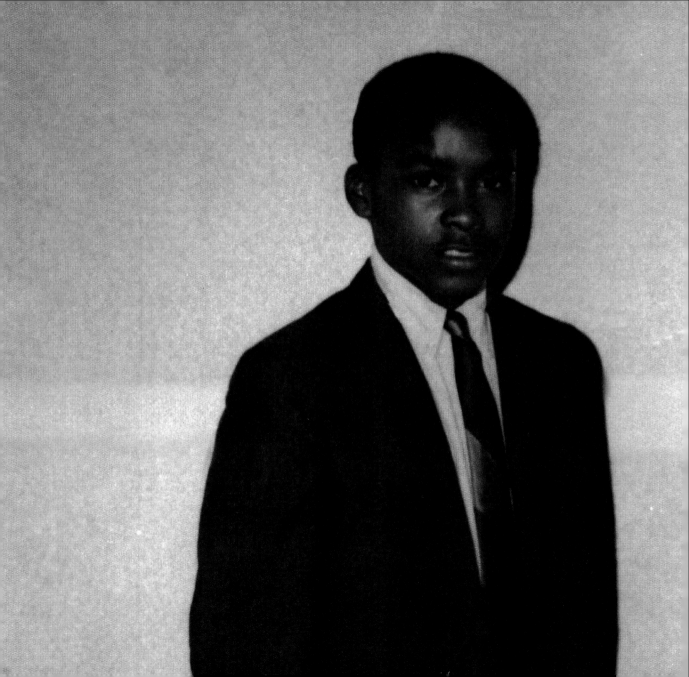

Big Took

As a teen living in South Central Los Angeles, I lifted weights to make my muscles big. They grew so large my **homeboys** (HOME-boyz), or friends, called me "Big Took."

Back then, very few kids carried guns, knives, or any other weapon. We thought we were tough enough. We didn't need weapons.

◀ *Tookie didn't always have big muscles. He decided to lift weights to look tough.*

5

Dodging Bullets

One day Raymond Washington and I started a gang called the Crips. We wanted to protect our families and friends from other violent gangs. Crips were good fighters. But other gangs started using guns. Everywhere we went, we had to duck and dodge bullets. The Crips thought the only way we could protect ourselves and prove we were tough was to use guns too.

When gangs use guns, no one is safe. ▶

Guns Everywhere

Carrying and using guns became the "**down**" (DOWN) thing to do. Kids who weren't good fighters felt strong and tough and cool when they carried guns.

The streets of South Central became even more violent. Gangs started shooting and killing other gangs. They used guns to rob stores and when they sold drugs. We thought guns would make us safer. Instead, they made things worse.

◀ *In many neighborhoods guns are everywhere. They only make things worse.*

Losing My Homeboys

My homeboy Raymond was killed by a gang member who was afraid of him. My closest and best homeboy, Buddha, was also killed. I still miss him.

I have lost more of my homeboys to guns and violence than you can count on all your fingers and toes. They are dead because gang members killed them with weapons.

It hurts a lot to lose someone close to you because of gang violence. ▶

Muscles Don't Stop Bullets

Since I had big muscles and a big **reputation** (rep-you-TAY-shun), I thought no one could hurt me.

But my big muscles and big reputation couldn't stop the bullets that a gang member fired at me one day. Doctors said I would never walk again. It took a long time, but I can walk now.

I don't want you to get shot too. That's why I'm telling you my story. You can learn from my mistakes.

◄ *Many gang members end up in wheelchairs because they were shot.*

Becoming Old Too Soon

Weapons and violence create a lot of sadness and death. Even when you act as if violence doesn't bother you, it does. You worry about the families of the people you hurt. You worry about what will happen to you because you hurt others.

You may be young, but you'll have a lot to worry about if you walk around hurting people.

People who hurt others always have to worry about being hurt themselves. ▶

Do or Die

"Do or Die" has been the Crips' **motto** (MOT-toe) since we started. "Do or Die" means to do whatever is necessary to defend your **'hood** (HOOD)—your neighborhood— or your gang, even if it means you have to die doing it.

Raymond and I had no idea that there were other ways to deal with violence. Now I know. But it's too late for Raymond.

◄ *Some gangs use weapons to protect their neighborhoods from other gangs. This does more harm than it does good.*

Don't Carry Guns

Many kids carry guns like we did. Some kids bring them to school. A lot of kids say they carry a gun for protection, to defend themselves. Other kids carry guns to show how down they are. Some kids even believe that carrying guns makes them grown-up.

Kids think they have lots of reasons to carry guns. But there are no good reasons. They all lead to violence, death, and sadness.

Even carrying a toy gun to school puts everyone at risk. ▶

A Real Grown-Up

As a kid, you're still growing up. You'll learn a lot of things as you become an adult. You'll learn how to take care of yourself. You'll learn how to be fair with others, and how important it is to tell the truth. You'll learn how to make good choices that don't get you or other people into trouble.

You'll also learn that carrying a gun won't make you a grown-up. Being violent won't make you a grown-up. The only thing violence does is get you shot, killed, or put in jail.

◀ *You can learn how to make good choices from adults who love you.*

Become a True Hero

Most kids who carry guns and shoot people feel scared inside. They're afraid of what other kids will think of them if they walk away from an argument or a fight. So they carry guns.

Real tough and strong kids stay away from guns. They're true **heroes** (HERE-ohs) because they're brave. Heroes know right from wrong. They don't let anyone push them into hurting themselves or others.

Glossary

to be **down** (DOWN) To be ready to do anything, no matter how dangerous, because your homeboys expect it of you.

hero (HERE-oh) Someone who is truly brave and strong and doesn't need to use weapons.

homeboy (HOME-boy) Friend or partner.

'hood (HOOD) Slang for neighborhood.

motto (MOT-toe) Words to live by.

reputation (rep-you-TAY-shun) What people think about you.

Index